'This is a moving (
bright young talent w
of hardship. As one
poetry throughout
inspiration and solace it can give. Everyone, especially
if they feel troubled or anxious, will find this book
an invaluable source of comfort and know
they are not alone.'

Marjorie Wallace CBE FRCPsych
Founder and Chief Executive of SANE

To my mum

Thank you for never giving up, always having hope
and empowering me to take on the world!

SAMANTHA CRILLY

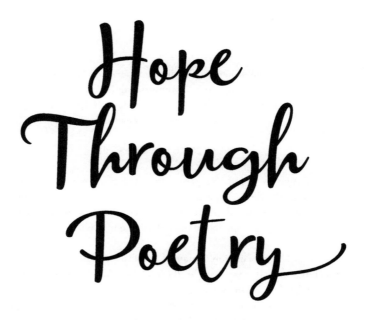

Hope
Through
Poetry

Poems for resilience
and self-esteem

Foreword by Neil Long

With illustrations by Barnaby Tompkins

Hammersmith Health Books
London, UK

First published in 2020 by Hammersmith Health Books
– an imprint of Hammersmith Books Limited
4/4A Bloomsbury Square, London WC1A 2RP, UK
www.hammersmithbooks.co.uk

British Library Cataloguing in Publication Data:
A CIP record of this book is available from the British Library.

Print ISBN 978-1-78161-168-5
Ebook ISBN 978-1-78161-169-2

Commissioning editor: Georgina Bentliff
Design: Madeline Meckiffe
Cover design: Madeline Meckiffe
Cover and inside illustrations: Barnaby Tompkins
Index: Hammersmith Books Limited
Production: Helen Whitehorn, Pathmedia
Printed and bound by: TJ International Ltd, Cornwall, UK

Contents

»→ ✷ ←«

Foreword

Samantha Crilly is a powerhouse. And an inspiration. I could fill a whole page with positive words about this one. In fact, the whole family are quite extraordinary; I have become a family friend over the years, so it is a pleasure and an honour to write this foreword for Samantha's new book.

Poetry can sometimes communicate more than plain text or even a good story. It comes from a deeper place, and if you relax and soak it up enjoyably, I think you will get the depth of what Samantha is communicating. I think this allowance of a free-flowing imagination plus her performing arts have been key in Samantha's healing process.

When I first encountered Samantha's poetry, I was thinking thoughts along the lines of 'Old Soul' or 'She's been here before!'

Anyway, you can decide.

On a practical level, I think this book has many good uses. If you are a carer or a sufferer, these poems can give you an insight into mental issues without having to read a dry and heavy-going textbook, plus, as the reader you are provided with a safe, non-judgemental space to explore your own thoughts and emotions. A non-judgemental space to just Be is so important.

Societal issues are touched on, like social media, and the message that 'It's okay not to be okay' comes through loud and clear. Also, each poem leaves you with a happy and hopeful message.

Get stuck into these. Enjoy. And love and cherish your mental health.

Neil Long
Voice and Confidence Coach
Radio Presenter and Broadcaster, Family Friend

How to use this book

So how should you use this book? First of all, please enjoy it. Thumb the pages, find the verses that resonate particularly with you, and take some comfort, strength and, I hope, inspiration from the words I have written. Use the 'My thoughts…' pages to make your own notes. Add doodles or diagrams, underline the lines that leap out at you, and write your own responses to the questions and issues I raise. In short, make this book your own. I hope you will come back to it again and again and perhaps, as time goes on, you'll tweak those notes and doodles or find that different poems appeal. Please take this book on your own journey – I hope it goes with you to some wonderful and surprising places.

Samantha Crilly

My story

»——➤✦←——«

Thank you for taking the time to look at this book and to read my poetry. I hope that you will take a positive message from my writing, recognising that a glimmer and shimmer of light can be found even through dark and challenging times.

Writing this book has been a cathartic experience for me, helping me find a way to express thoughts and words that can often be hard to say out loud. Committing my feelings to paper calms me, helps me unravel difficult emotions, and also shows me just how far I have come. I hope reading my verses will help you in a similar way.

Writing poetry has been a helpful, healthy way of organising the sea of emotions I have often felt adrift in. Over the years I have expressed these feeling through far more destructive paths. From the age of 13, I spiralled into the grip of an eating disorder which put a huge strain on both me and my family throughout my teenage years. Then, as I felt that recovery was almost within my reach, I swapped one mental illness for another, becoming ill with obsessive compulsive disorder. Once again the order I sought eluded me, and my life felt very out of control.

Finally in my mid-20s, with the unwavering support of my family and friends, I found two great passions – drama and poetry – both giving me a creative outlet and a home for my imagination which was crucial to my recovery. I began a degree in stage and media, and as I became happier and more self-confident, I also became much more committed to writing. I can now look back and see that as each poem took shape and form, I moved a little further forward towards long-lasting health and happiness.

To be here now, as the author of this book, feels quite wonderful and exciting. I hope that all who read it will find strength and understanding through its pages. I am not an academic, nor a trained writer; I am simply a young woman writing from the heart about real things that matter to me, and some have said that is the most powerful thing about my poetry.

I have enjoyed writing this so much and I hope that comes across to those who read it. I hope it shows that if you believe in yourself and your recovery, then you can move forward. Those steps you take may be tiny, but they add up over time and now, in a much healthier place, I can see how far I have come. Sometimes I feel frustration that there is still a little way to go, but if I have learnt anything, it is that this journey cannot be rushed.

I am so incredibly grateful to all those who have encouraged me to get here and have let me follow my own path at my own pace, which has led to this book that you are holding in your hands today. Fifteen years ago, in the grip of anorexia nervosa, I hardly dared to think about the future. From that dark, frightening place I could never have imagined the sunshine that I would be standing in now.

Acknowledgements

»——→ ⚜ ←——«

I would like to say a big thankyou to my incredible mum and dad for always believing that recovery was possible and for giving me the freedom to follow my dreams.

Charlotte, my loyal and loving twin sister for being the wind beneath my wings.

Jay, your unconditional love has been the final piece in my puzzle.

My wonderful grandparents, thank you for loving me the way you do, mental illness and all!

Callum for being the brother I never had and always being there.

To my Aunty Sue and Uncle Steve for always being a phone call away.

A special thankyou to Zoe, Kim, Hannah, Alice, Maisie, Ed, Maria and all my friends for being everything a friend could want and more.

To Neil, who from the very beginning has joined me on my creative journey and encouraged me to be me.

A warm thank you to my wonderful GPs, past and present, John Dalzell and Sarah Benney, who over the years have always given me their unreserved support.

Thank you to Barnaby for bringing my poems alive through his brilliant illustrations.

Over the years I have been incredibly blessed
to have been supported by so many wonderful people,
including Dave Spinx, Carina Skinner, Mitch,
Aunty Kate, Dionne and Leanne.

Last and by no means least, thank you to my
lovely publisher Georgina Bentliff (Hammersmith Health
Books) for being so supportive, open-minded and a total
pleasure to work with.

Once again, a big thank you to all those mentioned above and
the many others who have championed, helped and supported
me over the years; without each and every one of you, I know
I would not be who and where I am today… Thank you!

Introduction

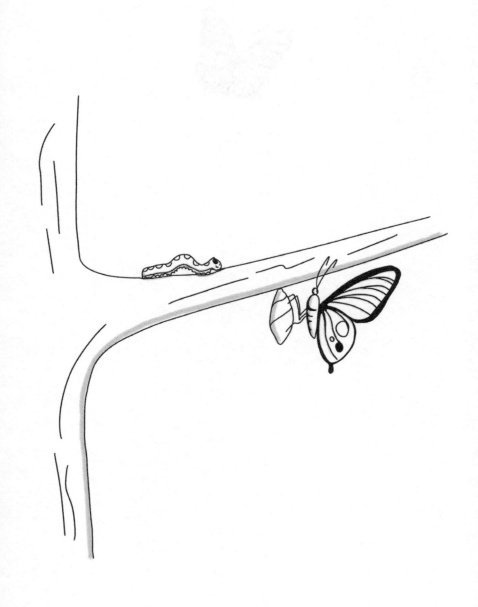

Hope

Mental illness is like a cancer of the mind,
An imperceptible indiscriminate presence in humankind.
Those touched by it will know it's a debilitating living
nightmare
But even in our deepest darkest moments of despair
Though we may not always see hope, it doesn't mean it
it isn't there.
The purpose of this book is to give you, the reader, an insight
into mental illness through both a sufferer's and their
carers' eyes,
To undo everything surrounding mental illness that has been
strongly stigmatised,
But most of all to shine a light on recovery and the peace you
can still find,
The rebuilding of love and relationships which were once
left behind.
Please remember that there is always a way out, for all of you –
This book will have fulfilled its purpose when you eventually do.

Family

My thoughts

A hand to help

»—→↯←—«

A poem from an outsider's point of view

I can see you through my window, struggling upstairs,
Your family beneath you, blissfully unaware,
Just a ceiling between you not knowing your pain,
A concept any family would never wish to entertain.
I know you have pride and that's why you hide,
That this is the reasoning behind your lonesome divide.
If only you knew, they would be up there with you,
Holding your hand,
Wanting to understand.
I wish I could tell you it will be okay,
That you're no burden to be feeling this way.
However, we both know silence will never get you past
the door,
That all these secrets won't lift your knees up off the floor.
Please hold out your hand for people to listen,
To accept help and free yourself from this villainous prison.

A mother's love

»———→ ↯ ←———«

A poem about my Mum

A feeling so spiritual, so unique
It watches over me when I sleep,
Catches the bad dreams before they land,
Strengthens me as it holds my hand,
Surrounding me with love and hope,
Putting faith inside me when I can't cope.
By my side for when my demons appear,
Be my shield for when they come near
To die before me holding no fear…
Some say it's an angel looking down from above
But I know it's down here… it's my mother's love.

Dedicated to my amazing mum

My thoughts

Charlotte

»——→⚘←——«

A poem about my twin sister

When I was dragged into the depths of hell
My sister jumped in after me and we both fell.
Grabbing my hand as we hit the ground
She pulled me to my feet as we both looked around.
I could see the fear seeping from her eyes
As I began to turn into a monster she no longer recognised.
Imprisoned in a place so cold and hollow,
She had the gateway to turn back but she would always follow.
Protecting me was something she was determined to do –
She just kept repeating the words 'I will never leave you'.
She didn't. She stayed by my side all the way through
Even when I was too blind to say 'thank you'.
Not once has she blamed me for bringing her down to such a place,
Not once did she throw back any of her losses in my in face.
I wanted to write this poem for carers, siblings and friends
Who often get forgotten until the horror ends.
Every sufferer is thankful and really does love you –
They are just riddled with an illness that doesn't trust you,
But when your loved ones come back into the light
Your bond will be unbreakable and will shine the brightest of
bright

Dedicated to my beautiful twin sister x

Dad

My dad , the epitome of black and white thinking –
If you smoke, just stop smoking…
If you drink, just stop drinking…
What a simple way of viewing it – if only we all could
Wouldn't life be a lot more straightforward?
By no means has he had an easy life; quite the opposite in a way
But he's always had a 'normal' brain as I like to say.
Then I come along, riddled with mental illness,
A big illogical, bizarre Mess…
Yet he has never made me feel less of a person.
We may joke about it sometimes, but I've never felt like
anyone's burden
Even if I asked him to do the most absurd thing he has ever done
If it helped me feel safe, it would in a second be done
And just knowing he would do that for you
Is all he has to do.

To my lovely dad x

My thoughts

My willow tree

»——→ ⚘ ←——«

A poem about my Grandma

Having the power of her time on this earth
To set fire to my ambitions and know my self-worth
She may not always agree or understand this new era
But she accepts that time will always interfere,
Changing everything she once knew –
That's the beauty of how our unique friendship grew,
Colliding our worlds together, making one we both share,
A place we breathe both old and new air,
Refusing to conform, creating our own norm of madness
Talking so openly about happiness and sadness,
A place with no judgement, to be utterly free
My best friend, my very own willow tree.

For my wonderful Grandmary

Other relationships

My thoughts

I miss you

A poem about separation

If I could, I would fly over and kiss you,
Whisper in your ear how much I've missed you.
I know your loneliness has peaked higher than you're used to.
I would have visited but this time I refuse to
Even though it breaks my heart
To spend all this time apart,
Time will always have a way of passing,
Leaving no moment we own ever-lasting.
Our time will soon come back around –
Then I can hold you in my arms safe and sound.

I'll be

A poem for carers

I wish I could feel the pain that aches you,
The grip of the presence which constantly takes you,
The sound of these voices which always wake you.
I know I have always been the one you look to,
Yet this time around there is nothing I can do.
What you're going through I will never completely
understand;
However, I can still sit next to you and listen
with no judgement in hand,
Tell you every day how much the world needs you,
Be the angel on your shoulder for when the illness
misleads you.
I'll be the good in your bad
The happy in your sad.
I'll be the worst enemy your illness has ever had.

Dancing demons

»——→✦←——«

A poem about mental illness
in a relationship

I always knew there would be something living alongside
you and me,
Something you had warned me about and how capable it
could be.
I too had kept secrets, hidden behind closed doors.
'I understand,' I pledged, 'I can help you with yours'.
Convinced my demons had been put to sleep,
Little did I know, they weren't sleeping deep –
Simply waiting for some friends to help them back on their
feet.
At first it didn't show its face too often
But this soon changed as our love started to blossom.
You began to share more and more secrets about it
Like it leering in corners if you had fun without it.
I walked in on you ripping carpet out of the floor,
Hearing you systematically move furniture through the door –
It had now become the three of us: it, you and me,
'It' being the beast you worshipped, called OCD.
But what could I say? I was besotted with you
Whilst *my* demons awakening soon became due.
Holding your hand whilst the darkness loomed,
Watching our demons dance in the middle of the room.

Suffering for them was like sweet perfume –
We lived alongside them making it work for a while
But I knew I had to give up this love-struck denial
'My darling,' I confessed, 'our demons dance too well,
Re-opening up my gates to hell,
Somewhere I know only too well.'
My love for you was a painful sacrifice I had to swallow
But I knew if I didn't let you go, the monsters
would always follow.

The rays of the sun

»——→ ✦ ←——«

A poem about mental illness
in a relationship

Sometimes I think I can see the water clearly,
I can see your reflection, but I can't feel you near me.
I look down at the golden sand,
I grab it and hold it but it slithers through my hands.
I think back to when we first met, flying high, burning bright –
Now so cold, falling deep into the night.
When I walk into the darkness, I can hear your mumbles,
Slight movement too, as I feel your tumbles.
I know deep down inside you want me to be with you
But the night always lasts longer than we want it to.
Right now, I need to live under the rays of the sun;
I will keep praying that one day you will finally come.

My thoughts

The smile

»——→ ✢ ←——«

A poem about checking in
with your loved ones

You can tell by their eyes they are haunted,
Home to a presence severely unwanted,
Lips stretched wide, cheeks tense and plump,
Planning that night to take the jump.
Feel the wind crash against their face
In the hope of arriving at a more peaceful place.
They are funny – they always were,
Using playfulness as their protective armour,
Building it and building it until they crack inside.
It's never a long-lasting place to hide.
How can they look so happy? I can't understand why?
The ones with the loudest laugh can be the quietest to cry.
Watch out for those ones – they whisper silently,
Often suffering in this bitter irony.
Check up on that friend you haven't seen in a while,
The one who always wears a magnificent smile –
They may have needed you in that very moment
To save them from their soul they would have otherwise
broken.

Window pain

»——————◊——————«

A poem from the outside looking in

It's as if I'm watching you through a glass pane,
Grieving at the thought of never meeting you again.
All I want to do is reach you
But my words never seem to make it through.
I know you're in agony, that your good days are very few,
But is it selfish of me to say that it hurts me too?
To love someone so madly
Yet have something this evil take you away so gladly?
I hope you know
I will always be here for when the cracks start to show,
When the pane smashes to the floor
And you arrive back on this side of the door?
I am here for you
To hold you, to love you, to help you through
What seems like an endless maze.
Even in your darkest days
I will cease to leave your side,
I will sit beside you when you hide
And we will get through this together –
Please just don't leave me waiting back here forever.

My thoughts

Zoe

A poem about friendship

During my illness, I lost many friends through no fault
of their own –
We were young and innocent, how could they possibly
have known
I had become subject to an illness that wanted me silent
and alone?
It made sense to walk away.
They knew a nightmare was looming as a consequence to stay.
But I was so lucky to have one who did,
Always finding me in my darkest hour when I hid.
She stood next to me in times of hopelessness and confusion,
The friend she once knew was now just a vacant illusion,
Giving me everything when I was unable to give back,
Never questioning the love to her in which I lacked.
We never spoke about the illness – we didn't have to –
She always had an unspoken understanding of what a friend
should do,
And now finally my eyes are open wide enough to say
'thank you'.

For my best friend Zoe Shellie

My thoughts

Freedom

A poem about being in the right relationship

Freedom is often dreamt of by many, if not all –
A gift which can open our worlds that may at times feel so small.
Whether it be physical freedom – being able to travel the
world –
Financial freedom – holding more notes than you've ever held –
Or something as simple as feeling safe crossing the street
Without being afraid of any monsters you might meet…
For me, it has always been my mind,
Endlessly keeping me entwined.
I longed for the freedom to love something more than I loved *it*,
To perhaps start to break its rules just a little bit.
Then I met you, and what a world you brought me into,
Helping me to break each rule one by one,
Holding me in your arms after each one was done.
We faced all my demons and diminished them together.
You whispered, I'll do it for as long as it takes, even if it takes
forever.

To my lovely Jay

Illness

In my head

>——→ ⚓ ←—«

A poem about OCD

Wow, I didn't sleep well last night
Although, for me, I guess it was alright…
Wait, did I leave the plug on at Jess's?
Of course, don't need to keep on with second guesses…
Checked it ten times while I was there
Although distracted on what to wear –
Too many colours clash with my hair…
Must have the same colour, keep it simple,
Too many colours confuse me, must be minimal.
Darn, mermaid ornament has moved place –
Need to put back, just in case.
What is wrong with my face?
Three spots? Must have four…
Oh, did I check the lock on the door?
One two three four five six seven eight nine ten…
Wait one minute, let me check again.
One two three four five six seven eight nine ten…
Let go of it now, I'm late for school
But first must touch dark spot on wall.
Touch ten times, then with elbow…
Mustn't touch the other one… Bugger, I'm too low
Get in the middle, right there you go…
I'm now three hours late –
Don't let anyone see me lick the school gate…

What if…?

»—→—⁂—←—«

A poem about OCD
(obsessive compulsive disorder)

OCD can be very much based on the 'what if…?'
What if I didn't switch the light off?
But I did… but then again, I may not have…
Did I put all my ornaments back in the right place?
Yes, but maybe I should go back and check just in case?
OCD thrives on totally confusing the mind;
It continuously loves blurring the lines;
Endless questioning…
You know full well your can of beans
Hasn't magically merged into that tin of sardines.
Most of these things don't logically matter anyway –
You just listen to what the OCD will say.
It makes up consequences: some are small
But some can be lethal,
Such as your mum dying if you fail to turn off the plug
Or the whole world exploding if you don't
give that certain person a hug.
These sound crazy… but would you rather the 'tiny'
possibility of that happening?
Or you could just go back and check that light again?
Better not to have the burden of death for all those innocent
women and men…

I don't know if this poem makes any sense to onlookers trying
to keep their knowledge afloat
But one thing I can definitely say is, we are all very much in
the same boat.

My thoughts

My evil masterpiece

»—→⚜←—«

A poem about OCD

I can only describe it as a mould I had to fill,
A precious 'masterpiece' I'd slowly built –
Years of creating its intricate design
Soon became the sole purpose of mine.
Even though it was, well… a big load of nothingness
Yet fitting inside it, indoctrinated, I was at my best.
Every single edge I'd drawn, every barrier I'd built,
Was simply standing down to my own empty guilt,
Convinced that if I ever destroyed it, I'd be left with
no meaning
This is where OCD can be so blindly deceiving.
None of the rules I had constructed made any sense,
I just kept adding to my 'masterpiece' at my own expense.
My purpose wasn't to live for a structure that had ceased
to exist,
To abide by every rule and fulfil every wish –
I knew if I'd created it, I could also knock it down
And, believe me, it felt truly liberating when it finally hit
the ground.
I became free
And, let me tell you, I've never been more happy.

My thoughts

The plum

»——→✤←——«

A poem about OCD

I'm standing in a fruit shop deliberating on what to buy…
Most of it doesn't even go with my head,
far too many colours is why.
A green apple fits best so I'll grab that one there…
THEN an enthusiastic fruiterer pops out of nowhere.
Fruiterer: Can I help you at all?
Me: No, don't worry, I'm just going to get an apple.
Fruiterer: Oh okay, do you like lots of fruit then?
Me: Yes, I love it… *(it just depends when)*
Fruiterer: Well, in that case, we have some tasty plums.
Me: Oh…
Fruiterer: Here, these ones…
Me: Oh yes, they look nice, but I don't need any today.
Fruiterer: Not to worry – you can try one anyway!
Me: That's very kind of you, but really I'm okay…
Fruiterer: Oh, go on! Here, you can have one for free.
Me: (*blubber comes out of my mouth as he
stares back at me*)
Do you know what, I'll eat it in a minute
(*even though it's already sitting in my hand*)
Fruiterer: It's clean. I'd like to know what you think.
I grew it on my land. They are nice and soft…
Me: …Oh for god's sake, why can't you just
SOD THE SOD OFF!

An invasion

>——❧——<

A poem about pure 'O'
(obsessive compulsive disorder)

I want to talk about a form of OCD called Pure O
Where one can encounter thoughts unlike the person we all
know,
Thoughts that to another mind may seem insane
Such as obsessive counting or inflicting pain,
Often on your loved ones again and again.
The earliest compulsion I remember was as a little girl
I began to have these absurd thoughts but would never tell,
Torturing myself within my own mind, I hid them very well,
Sat there, holding a small baby in my living room.
I should have been in my element one would assume
But all I could think about was throwing the baby into the fire,
Obsessing over this, I despised myself for having such a sick
desire,
Telling myself these thoughts weren't real, I felt like a stone-
cold liar.
I convinced myself I was evil, or was I going mad?
Punishing myself for every preposterous thought I ever had:
Urges such as jumping out of a car on the motorway,
Then thinking of that slight moment of unknowingness all day…
How can I have this compulsion yet absolutely detest having it,
Having no actual legit reasons for pursuing it?

Until I came to know it was a common form of OCD called
Pure O...

'Someone who experiences obsessive, unwanted thoughts
with no visible compulsions to perform,
Often referred to as intrusive thoughts far from the norm...'
To anyone despising themselves for what enters their head
Think of it as an alien intrusion of forceful thoughts instead
Without which the OCD would otherwise be dead.
You can overcome them, and always push through,
Just trust in what is the OCD and what is really you.

An unwanted intruder

»——→✦←——«

A poem about OCD
(obsessive compulsive disorder)

I lay there asleep, in peace on my bed
Avoiding waking to confront the demon in my head,
Losing myself in my beautiful dreams,
Feeling free, well, for what it seems.
I wake and feel the constraint around me,
Face to face with the monster that has found me,
Reeling out a list of rules I should follow,
Each with a meaning that seems so hollow.
But as I do one, it makes me do more —
If I ever missed one, it would yell as it saw…
I obeyed every rule, scared of upsetting it;
It knew it could own me, and I was letting it.
Drained and tired
From doing what it desired,
I was the personal slave it had hired.
So consumed in the rituals I had to do
I was losing everything else that once was true.
My freedom was jailed
Imprisoned in a hell I hailed.
Watching my loved ones fall apart beside me,
It was time I set light to the fire inside me.
This presence was my enemy, not my friend,
And a relationship that I needed to end.

I burnt my bridges and cut my ties,
I ripped it apart and said my good-byes.
I have the freedom now to live my life and be free
But over my shoulder, it's always watching me.
Its shadow lingers at a distance
And whispers to me in its persistence,
But I stand strong...

My thoughts

The silent scream

»—→ ⚜ ←—«

A poem about self-harm

Floating through mid-air I can't feel a thing
Sitting here swaying on a motionless swing –
So many emotions I can't seem to translate:
Pressure, rage, guilt, confusion and hate.
Losing grip of gravity, I fall to the floor
Pressing down on myself, I can't feel anymore.
How do I connect to the world again?
I'll do anything, even if it's through pain,
But this will only serve as a short-term distraction –
I know full well I will always get the same brief reaction.
Like everything that is temporary, the pain soon subsides
As my demons instantly slither back inside –
A vicious cycle I spend my whole life trying to hide.
But I do have a choice –
I was given a voice.
I can either sit here in silence, or I can ask for help.
I can struggle in the dark or I can speak out.
And when I do
This will be when the rays of the sun start shining through.

My thoughts

From a sufferer to a sufferer

»——→ ᵥ ←——«

A poem from me to you

I purged on the control.
Its gratification was preposterous,
A monstrous high, fuelling my soul purpose
Of becoming… becoming… what?
An emaciated version of myself who'd completely lost the plot?
Anorexia had structure and it had rules,
Whilst relishing in taking me for a fool,
Brainwashing me with success
Whilst pulling me deeper into its villainous mess.
I was never in control; I was being controlled
Whilst unknowingly waiting for my death to unfold.
The only moments of my control were when I was fighting
against it
As much as the illness stood against me to prevent it.
From a sufferer to a sufferer,
The only thing you are succeeding in is losing everything –
Your freedom, your friends and your family –
That's the stone cold truth.
I know it's repulsively ugly…
Use that strength you give to anorexia in your recovery.
I was always so petrified of what recovery would be
When the truth is, you're just setting yourself free.

Pure

»—→⚜←—«

A poem about orthorexia

I knew if I did enough research, I'd find the cure,
The healthiest way to live life clean and pure –
Then I could reach the very peak of my existence.
I'd be able to defy ageing and illness with enough persistence.
I began looking at nutrition in depth, studying endless books;
I gradually started to change and began to like the way I looked,
But of course, I'm one of those people that are all or nothing –
I'll do anything to achieve my goals whilst inhaling the suffering.
I started to follow every detail of nutrition intensely,
Counting every single nutrient to its tee;
If I went a little bit under or over, I was convinced it would
harm me.
I was fixated on eating an array of colours in a rainbow
Because I had read it would give me that youthful glow.
Every single nutrient had to reach its full criteria.
No one else was doing it, so it would make me superior.
If anyone even suggested I step outside of my strict routine
Fear would shoot up my spine at the thought of it not being clean.
I knew socialising took place around eating and drinking;
Colleagues would ask me to come after work without even
thinking,
Never taking into account the nutritional requirements of my
evening meal –
How dared they! What were they trying to do? Make me ill?!
To me today, this sounds absolutely absurd

And to you it may be the craziest thing you've ever heard?
I was fixated on reaching optimal health and so frightened of
messing it up.
My inner soul had given up.
I was just living for food…
Food over my friends, food over my family, food over my life

—

Since when did my distortion of food become so rife?
This wasn't 'optimal health' —
If anything I was sick. I was thin, I was tired
Of slaving away
Every single day
To reach the exact elements my body 'required'.
I was failing to include everything my heart had desired
So now I go by this simple rule…
Eat to nourish your body, but also to nourish your soul;
They work hand in hand to make you a flourishing whole.

Beauty not the beast

»——→⚜←——«

A poem about
body dysmorphia disorder

I'm a monster, undeserving to be here.
I know you're terrified in case I come near.
I'll infect you with my gorging ugliness.
I can see you through my sunken eyes in all their puffiness.
Of course, everyone's going to stare
At my asymmetrical face I hide behind my hair.
My body is inhuman; it wasn't made like yours.
Just looking at it is the worst pain one can endure,
Yet people say I'm beautiful. I can't understand why —
To me it's just a made up pitiful lie.
…This is what I used tell myself every single day —
Ugly, disgusting, repulsive, were the only words I could say.
When we listen to ourselves long enough, it can become our
reality.
I slowly began to change it, I started to tell myself I was
beautiful,
That maybe the strangers next to me weren't laughing to be
cruel.
Maybe they were laughing at an inside joke between them all?
The elderly man was never staring at me because I was vile;
He just wanted to share a friendly mutual smile?
And perhaps the compliments are because I *am* beautiful
And maybe, just maybe, I really am meant to be here after all?

Changing my perspective on myself was never going to be a
quick magical cure
But it did give me that first step to recovery I had always
hoped for.

Ana

»———→ ❦ ←———«

A poem about
anorexia nervosa (eating disorder)

Sitting down to my family dinner,
Everyone staring as I become thinner.
Ana slowly creeping into my thoughts
Telling me to put down my knife and fork.
There's nothing I can do to make her eat, Mum
whispers to Dad.
Ana smiles, all smug and glad.
I don't understand why she won't eat, Dad mutters to Mum.
Secret is I do – I'm just wrapped around Ana's thumb.
Feeling my bones rub against the chair
Even through all the layers I wear,
Running upstairs and locking my door
Drained and exhausted I collapse on the floor.
Ana, you're killing me, I can't let you win.
I take off my top and see my heart beat through my skin.
Mum and Dad banging on the door,
I whisper to Ana I don't want you anymore –
I'm going to die if you win this war!
You're nothing without me Ana cries –
Another one of her crazy lies.
Ana will always find a way of creeping into your mind,
Brainwashing you, making you blind,
Unable to see what you are doing to your body,

To her it is just an evil hobby.
To those she has touched and lived within,
Please, please, do not let her win.
Hers is a corrupt and vicious mind.
To make yourself happy, it is not her but you, you must find.

My thoughts

The nearest star

»——→❧←——«

A poem about dementia

Witnessing you to be ripped of your soul
Soon made me realise, we are all just shells after all
Housing what truly makes us all human —
A casing perceived as a lifelike illusion
Soon diminishes when stripped of the soul it's been using.
How can I grieve for you whilst you stare back at me
Gazing blankly? You no longer see
The memories we once shared when you were free.
A distant absence now lingers behind your eyes
As I become a stranger you no longer recognise,
But I will always sit next to you holding your hand
As I still have this part of you left on this land,
To love and to hold,
To keep warm when it's cold.
I know your soul will never be far,
Just waiting for me on the nearest star.

Behind the mask

»—→ ✲ ←—«

A poem about depression

People sometimes ask me why I feel this way
And for the life of me I can never think of what to say.
It can be mistaken for a feeling of sadness, but this couldn't
be less true,
Although, don't get me wrong, I can feel sad too.
I can even feel streaks of happiness run through my mind
But it's always the clarity I can never seem to find.
Like an emotionless fog running through my head space,
Always keeping me in exactly the same place,
An intense crippling timeless dimension
Where everything I do requires constant attention.
It sounds crazy, but the biggest struggle for me is getting out
of bed –
It's never out of laziness; it's pure dread for the day ahead.
An ongoing battle which continuously waits at my feet,
The same one as yesterday I crawled my way through
to defeat.
The only escape I encounter is when I'm sleeping
Yet so often I still feel the depression slowly creep in.
I can occasionally be persuaded to venture out for a walk
But I pray I don't bump into anyone and have to talk.
Sometimes I catch familiar faces I haven't seen in a while
But I never set loose the truth, I just stand there and smile.
I do wonder if they can ever tell,
Then again I know my mask hides me well.

My home is now my safe place; I feel somewhat secure.
Nowadays I never really feel curious as to what's outside
the door.
I don't seem to hold a connection to the world anymore...
When I am in my moments of darkness
I always remember that time moves on regardless.
I know this present moment won't last after today
And maybe, just maybe, one day I will feel okay.

My thoughts

_____

_____

_____

_____

_____

_____

_____

_____

_____

_____

_____

_____

_____

_____

_____

_____

_____

_____

Dear Suicide

A poem about suicide

If we fly away together, can we go as high as we can?
So far away we'll lose sight of this land?
I have to admit it scares me ever so slightly —
I know life on this earth isn't given out lightly.
You've said it will be peaceful where we'll end up,
However, I've been told here many times I have too much to
give up.
I hope you're not lying as word says you're a thief
Wearing a mask of purity to cover the muck underneath.
You've made me swear not to listen to tomorrow
But it keeps telling me love still has time to grow,
That there is happiness down here still waiting for me,
That one day I will have the strength to set myself free,
So therefore, I've decided to pull out of our deal.
I know I'm worth so much more than how you feel.
Good-bye.
I hope you keep your thoughts to yourself
And I'm looking forward to sharing tomorrow with everyone
else.

Emotions

My thoughts

Monster on my back

>———✦←———«

A poem about carrying the heavy weight of a mental illness

It sat on my back quite comfortably most days,
Merrily playing along, singing my praise.
The taste of misery always kept it near
As it wined and dined lavishly on my fear.
I fed it for years, very generously so
It never had any motive to get up and go.
Only when I gradually stopped feeding it
Did it then grow weaker and weaker, the less I needed it.
Soon, having nothing to stay for
That's when it began to walk out of my door.
The stronger I grew, the weaker it became
As it starved profusely on the lack of my pain.
Light as a feather it soon blew away...
It can fly by my window from day to day
But I will always tell it to be on its way.

Loneliness

A poem about loneliness in the modern world

If we sent a text for every 'like' we made
It could have the capacity to cure a lonesome heartache.
If we smiled at one another as much as we do frown
Perhaps we would find ourselves looking up more instead
of down?
Or if we called someone the amount of times we 'liked'
their photos
It might just help them to carry on till tomorrow?
When we realise the power of human nature and
communication in the real world
We can start to bring back the comradeship and magic
we once held.

Hell in paradise

>——✿←—«

A poem about the torment
mental illness can bring

You can be in paradise yet in hell at the same time
Lying on a tropical beach yet still holding unrest inside.
Such peace the ocean brings to others never seems to override
The unpleasant hauntings that still lie by my side.
Like a pebble in my pocket, they go everywhere with me,
Negotiating my worth, always making it hard to see
That I do deserve good things in life without an apology.
None of us have to achieve anything to receive love from
others,
To be of a certain status or count money in high numbers.
Just to be human is enough to be loved in great amounts,
To have a kind soul and a generous heart is all that really
counts.

My thoughts

With angels you fly

≫——→🌱←——≪

A poem about grief

I gaze up at the birds as they pass on by,
Touching the rim of heaven beyond the sky –
Shoulder to shoulder with angels you fly.
I know now I can smile without having to justify
Being okay without you
Because I know you would want me to
Still laugh every day
And flourish in every way.
I had always held the burden of your absence in my mind,
Something you would have so wanted me to leave behind.
Even though it pains me to do so,
I know I have to let go,
Keeping all the wonderful memories of us together,
Gifts I now know will stay with me forever.

My thoughts

Glad you came

》—→ ⚜ ←—《

A poem about anxiety

It doesn't add up like it did with high-school mathematics
Or have a narrative to follow in morning amateur dramatics.
You can't find the square root of the problem, when the
problem doesn't exist
Or find reasoning for something when nothing was missed.
Anxiety manifests itself in so many different ways,
Often building and building over several days,
Detecting faults in situations that may never occur,
Preconditioning an event into one big blur,
Embarrassing yourself no matter what you do
On the main stage right in front of me and you,
Rubbing your knuckles, grinding your teeth,
Looking fine on the outside yet on fire beneath.
Heart pumping fast, echoing beats…
Dripping with sweat, hair slathered in grease,
Lungs tensed and twisted, unable to breathe –
If only you knew when you could leave.
But it's okay I whispered – leave as soon as you need;
I'm so proud of you for just coming along.
To have stayed even for a little while makes you so strong.

My guest: Anxiety

»—→✤←—«

A poem about anxiety
and friendship

Sorry I can't make it tonight. I already have a guest,
A different kind of one, unlike the rest.
It is unwanted, if that makes you feel any better?
Anxiety always decides when we can spend our time together.
Believe me, I'd much rather be with you,
But it never seems to allow our time together til it's long
overdue.
If I can, I'll pop by for an hour,
Although I may not talk much – I'll probably be drained of
brain power.
Still, I'd love to just sit quietly in your company.
Would that be okay? Just you and me?
If my guest comes knocking, we can chase it away together.
Watch on as it starts to crack under the pressure –
I bet if we did that long enough, it wouldn't come around
anymore.
It'll be walking and whispering straight past my door.
Shall we do that? Take the heat from its flame?
Leave it wondering why it ever came?

My thoughts

The voice

»——→✲←——«

A poem about the voice
of a mental illness

Some say it's a stranger's voice cursing in their ear
Others say it's the devil's words reducing them to tears
Others confess it's their own voice, a subconscious array of
fears…
The voice of a mental illness has always been undefined
But one thing it will never be, to a sufferer, is kind.

Society

Welcome to society

※—→⋎←—※

A poem about conditioning
in today's world

Hello and welcome to society, we hope that you enjoy your stay.
We will make it as relaxing as possible as long as you do things
our way.
First of all and most importantly, make sure you fix up your
exterior –
If you slack at any point we will soon make you feel inferior.
Secondly, your life will be controlled by pieces of paper –
We will count these up and decide how important you are later.
Thirdly, we want you to make your time here look as perfect
as possible;
Even if you're having a bad day this is not optional.
Fourthly, make sure you post every day on social media –
Once is fine at first, but we'll soon get needier.
In fact we can guarantee we'll be getting greedier and greedier.
Oh, and in terms of your meals,
We tend to advertise things to make you ill –
It keeps our drug companies going if you will.
Trust us, the more pills you pop, the better you'll feel …
Lastly, just so you know, our planet is on its way out
But it has to keep up with our needs so that's not something
we talk about.
So good luck and we hope everything is clear?
Oh, and don't smile too much – people will think you're weird.

What is 'normal'?

》—→ ⚘ ←—《

A poem about the
expectations of being normal

Normal is conforming to a certain standard, doing what is
conventional and expected.
Whatever the majority of people are doing around you is
automatically projected
Into who you think you should be, and if you aren't, it's
somewhat wrong,
Seen as a surprise when everyone else doesn't see you
following along,
Because what's normal seems to be a fixed image within
our minds
When in fact the definition has always been written through
blurred lines.
It's forever changing; the norm was so different years ago to
what it is today —
Even 50 years ago normality couldn't be further away…
The way we used to dress, behave and even talk.
Most youngsters today would rather take an uber than walk.
Kids never felt the pressure to set their statuses on 'likes' —
They were too busy playing in the park with their friends on
their bikes.
This has all changed now, meaning the word 'normal'
can be modified;
It can be revamped at any time,

But why wait for everyone else to decide?
You can do it, make it whatever you want it to be, something
that reflects you...
Whatever makes you thrive and be happy, that's what you
should do –
Dye your hair luminous pink, knit or eat out on your own,
Not drink alcohol or have social media lighting up your phone.
Perhaps you want to walk down the aisle in something bright
blue?
Well, I think you should go for it, because that's what normal
is for you.

My thoughts

Amity

»——→ ❧ ←——«

A poem about diversity

Life in general is such an absurd thing
So just have fun, never hesitate to spread your wings.
Whether you fit inside the arbitrary lines
Or erupt out of society's confines,
You are too magnificent to hide.
The day we see diversity as a gift,
That we can all be so different yet still coexist,
Will be the day we find true peace in this world,
But most importantly within ourselves.

My thoughts

Cyber friends

»——→↓←——«

A poem about the cyber world

I walked past you yesterday as we caught each other's eye.
We both knew it would have been weird if we had waved and
said hi,
So we walked on, looking back down at the same device we'd
been stalking each other on.

Peer pressure

»—→❧←—«

A poem about conforming

I have never really fitted in with the 'norm'
Though I spent all my teenage years feeling under pressure
to conform.
I worried so much about what everyone thought of me
I failed to be truly happy.
I felt like I was uncool because I didn't do what the 'it' girls
did –
I couldn't possibly just say 'I'm staying in tonight',
GOD FORBID!
I would sit and watch a movie which I should have technically
enjoyed
Yet I was too busy thinking I should be all the places I'd tried
so hard to avoid,
And even if I did go, I never enjoyed it anyway,
I just wish now I could go back in time and tell myself it's okay –
Stop being paranoid about people wondering why you're not
there
Because, truth be told, most of them don't really care –
They are too busy living their own lives to be that worried
about you.
So make sure you pursue whatever you want to do
And to be whoever you want to be
Because that is the only way you will ever be truly free.

Life

My thoughts

The unknown

»—→↓←—«

A poem about living each day
as if it's your last

Death has always possessed my veins with fear,
The unknowing as to whether it's far or near...
For something so natural, we don't talk about it much,
A subject often deemed too sensitive to touch.
Trying to grasp such a chilling reality...
Can be an inconceivable blessing we fail to see.
If we were made to live through eternity
Would life be precious or would we step out carelessly?
How long would it take us to ring up and say sorry?
Or see a long-lost friend in a hurry?
Or pursue that adventure if we didn't have to worry
About life being temporary?
None of us have the time of forever.
However, we do share this rare, extraordinary world together
And it's magical.
I don't know what will happen when I fall into the unknown
But I do know I'll be thanking everyone who made this planet
my home.

Keep me in reality

✤

A poem about the simple things in life

Yesterday I did something I hadn't done in a while –
I found myself unable to hold back a smile.
I looked up at the night sky and I was mesmerised by its beauty –
There were stars glistening, as the moon shone whole in all its duty.
I was frozen, swept away by everything I saw;
It crossed my mind, why hadn't I done this before?
Wondering if anyone still does this anymore?
Or are we so programmed to just stare at the floor?
I think, it started with my generation
As we are all glued to our iPhones and Play stations.
The next day I looked up at the sky for a second time –
Sapphire blue with a burning ball of fire warming those toes of mine,
Birds flying gracefully from tree to tree
As I listened to the gleaming river gently run by me.
We seem so focused on things which cease to exist
Such as how many social media 'likes' we can get on our list
Or how many Instagram posts have we missed?
Things that seem real and so important at the time…
Then it struck me, this was a sign

I'm failing to see the beauty which is already mine.
I asked my sister to lie beside me and gaze up at the stars;
Together we shared every single dream and ambition of ours.
I realised the things that really matter are already here in reality,
Somewhere I now know I will always want to be.

My thoughts

Covid 19

»——→❧←——«

A poem about our incredible workers

We all stood still for a moment in time,
Leaving the rat race instantly behind,
As Covid 19 took a hold of mankind.
Our first port of call was not our celebrities or the 'elite'
But the people we touch shoulders with every day in the
street,
Grinding tirelessly in jobs society downplays.
It was only then, when hardship came our way,
When all hope diminished out of sight,
That our true heroes stood in the spotlight.

My medicine

»——→ ✦ ←——«

A poem about what got me through my mental illness

Acting was my drug, a world I had to discover –
Once I had placed one foot in, I had no option but to recover.
My demons were silenced for that short space of time.
For what had always felt like a faraway dream of mine
Was soon obtainable every time I stepped inside –
Immeasurable people to be and places to see…
Somewhere I would never allow the illness to take away
from me.

My thoughts

Five minutes

»——→✣←——«

A poem about finding
the strength to get out of bed

It's within the first five minutes of waking –
Those five minutes lying there gazing at the ceiling,
deliberating
On whether the day is worth getting up for
Or if it's easier to once again close the door…
I'm always aware of the blessing to have another day
Yet the illness persists in taking it away.
However, I know if I can push myself just to get out of bed,
Wash myself down, brush my hair
Pick something to wear…
I know by that time, I'll be there…
As small as it sounds, this pocket of time
Is the deciding factor of mine
As to whether my days are stolen from me
Or I have the power to live them through and be free.

A filtered world

>——→⋅↯⋅←——«

A poem about the false
world of social media

It's hard to tell these days what is actually real —
Whether a happy face in a photo is how someone really feels.
A smile captured in a slight second;
Whether it was a human reaction or just beckoned?
The colours of the world once looked so true
Yet the filters now wash away the world that I knew.
It's been taken to somewhere unreachable, out of our grasp.
Even the ones living it struggle to make it last.
I still can't remember the point when a photo for myself
Then became one for everyone else,
When I first thought this world doesn't look bright enough —
I'll edit it here and there; how much can I bluff?
Or when I started to edit my face,
Trying to hide my flaws, which I used to embrace.
Well, everyone else's looked so much better than mine
I had to keep up with society, you know, keep in line,
But you soon realise when you get in the queue,
There is always, always someone in front of you,
Always looking like their life is so much better than yours
But we never consider what could be behind closed doors.
Just them, trying to carve the perfect life for everyone to
admire —

How many 'likes' can they instantly hire?
But as we all know, those will one day expire.
Our lives are spent worrying about how many 'likes' everyone
else is giving us
Yet we lose our time with everyone really living their lives
with us.
A photo used to be a pure memory taken for one's joy,
But now it's become everyone's guilty toy.
I once asked my grandma what she thought of this world;
She said, it has lost all the sincerity it once held.
A true picture is a memory in the heart –
It was pure, just for you; now that was art.

My thoughts

Bittersweet

»—→✤←—«

A poem about the good and bad life throws at you

When the air is sweet, I can rest my head;
A candied aroma always sends me to bed.
It's the bitter nights which provoke my unrest,
The ones where I find myself losing life's zest.
However, I know it's part of the deal life gave me –
It can't always hold out its hand and save me.
Life will always serve us bitter and sweet,
Otherwise it will never teach us to stand on our own two feet.
It will allow us to smoulder for a while under its heat,
But the butter always has to melt before its ready to eat –
Then its smooth richness will slather on our lips
As the problems of yesterday soon start to fix.
With a palate always receiving exactly the same
Perhaps life would soon become exceedingly plain?

The bigger picture

»——→🌿←——«

A poem about perspective

When you've hit rock bottom and made it out the other side
You find yourself taking life more in your stride.
Any small inconveniences that may now occur
No longer bother you, because you'll never be back where
you were.

Recovery

My thoughts

Game over

»———→✣←———«

A poem about recovery

Recovery isn't always going back to who you were before,
Meeting your exact same old self on the other side of the
door.
No one who's been through such chaos can come out unbled –
The mind will always evolve after such a battle inside one's
head.
That's the beauty of it, when coming out the other end –
You'll become a much stronger, wiser, forgiving version
instead.
It may not be perfect – moments of struggle still may re-visit –
But this time around you're in control of it.
That's what recovery is for me: I take hold of the reins;
Even if it still lingers near, my knees will never touch the
ground again.

My thoughts

Sink or swim

»——→ ✷ ←——«

A poem about the
challenges of recovery

We all have an inner strength, a reserve of faith,
In case we find ourselves on the edge of surrendering this
place.
It offers itself in times of desperation, when we lose all hope,
Giving us an extra dose of belief for when we just can't cope.
We will always have a choice as to if and when we use it,
Whether we grab it with both hands or own the willingness to
lose it.
You can either look at the world through eyes of venom and
resentment
Or have the courage to see a second chance for happiness and
contentment.
Believe that you can do it, that indeed you can win,
That the world doesn't want you to sink –
The world wants you to swim.

My thoughts

The answer

A poem about recovery from a mental illness

I heard there was somewhere I could go to set myself free,
Someone who had all the answers I'd need,
To grab a hold of the toil I found myself in,
Help to build me back up and thicken my skin.
I'd tried everything else till I was blue in the face —
It only ever took me to exactly the same place.
However, the next step I took wasn't such a mystery —
That place I'd been searching for was only ever me.
The situation I was in would never, by itself, set me free,
So I stopped deliberating on everything else I could do
Instead of actually doing the very thing I needed to…
As much as I tried to run and hide
I knew the answer lay only inside.

Finale

My thoughts

Accept to understand

》—→ ⚘ ←—《

A poem about accepting
the illogical mind of the sufferer

I had heard of anorexia before…
A mad concept – I didn't want to know more.
Someone severely malnourished, point blank refusing to eat
When I could have devoured it in a heart-beat?
To me, it was too irrational to even be a 'thing'.
Little did I know my ignorance would soon come back and
sting.
Years passed and anorexia came back into my thoughts,
But not through something I had read; instead we would talk.
Its ugly voice had worked its way deep inside my brain –
For something that seemed so obscene, my god, the pain!
I did things I never thought I would,
Performed rituals I never thought I could.
The sufferer I had heard about all those years ago, I now
understood –
Years battling an illness I thought would be a walk in the park
Brought me light from somewhere so very dark,
Opening my mind up to a whole new world
Where every judgement vanished that I had once held.
Even something I may not get
Should always have my utmost respect.
Now, if I come across something I don't understand

Instead of judging, I hold out my hand.
You may never truly know what someone else is going
through
But all you can do is hold out your hand too.

Resources

SANE

www.sane.org.uk
0300 304 7000 (4.30 pm – 10.30 pm daily)

SANE is a UK-wide charity working to improve quality of life for people affected by mental illness. SANE has three main objectives linked to its aims and outcomes:

To raise awareness and combat stigma about mental illness, educating and campaigning to improve mental health services

To provide care and emotional support for people with mental health problems, their families and carers as well as information for other organisations and the public

To initiate research into the causes and treatments of serious mental illness such as schizophrenia and depression and the psychological and social impact of mental illness.

SANE offers emotional support and information to anyone affected by mental health problems through its helpline and email services and its online Support Forum where people share their feelings and experiences.

Registered Charity Number: 296572

SAMARITANS

www.samaritans.org
Tel: 116 123 (UK) / 116 123 (ROI)

Samaritans offer a safe place for you to talk any time you like, in your own way – about whatever's getting to you. They are available round the clock, 24 hours a day, 365 days a year. If you need a response immediately, it's best to call Samaritans on the phone. This number is FREE to call.

Samaritans is a charity registered in England and Wales (219432) and in Scotland (SC040604).

BEAT

www.b-eat.co.uk
Helpline: 0845 634 1414

Beat is the UK's leading eating disorder charity and the largest of its kind in the world supporting people affected by eating disorders and campaigning on their behalf. It runs telephone helplines, local support groups and a website with information, message boards and online chat. Last year the charity had direct contact with 250,000 individuals, and many, many thousands more through its website and the media.

Registered Charity Number: 801343

ANXIETY UK

www.anxietyuk.org.uk
Info line: 03444 775 774 /
Text line: 07537 416 905

Anxiety UK work to relieve and support those living with anxiety and anxiety-based depression by providing information, support and understanding via an extensive range of services, including 1:1 therapy. They work regularly with external agencies and healthcare professionals to improve services for those living with anxiety and anxiety-based depression and also campaign to raise awareness of the conditions.

Registered Charity Number: 1113403

THE GRACE DEAR TRUST

www.thegracedeartrust.co.uk
Facebook: @gracedeartrust Twitter:
@GraceDearTrust1 Instagram: @gracedeartrust

The Grace Dear Trust is a Surrey-based Mental Health charity spreading and raising awareness around Surrey.

The Grace Dear Trust was set up in memory of Grace, who was a loving member of the Dear family and an amazing friend to many. She died in early 2017 after suffering from mental health problems for a number of years, in part falling victim to the inability to communicate her problems early enough or effectively enough to save her life. 'It's ok not to be ok'

Registered Charity Number: 1175955

THE FRANK BRUNO FOUNDATION

www.thefrankbrunofoundation.co.uk

0800 368 8196

'We are aiming to bring together the benefits of non-contact boxing with a solution focused well-being program. The aim is to bring healthy-body and healthy-mind approaches together to provide a holistic and enjoyable approach to supporting people with mental health problems. The aim is to help people to develop a healthier body and a healthier mind, building on their existing physical and emotional strengths and achievements. Our aspiration is that people will use the skills they learn on the programme to develop a happier, more fulfilling and successful future.'

Registered charity number: 1171012

ZERO SUICIDE ALLIANCE

www.zerosuicidealliance.com

The Zero Suicide Alliance is a collaborative of National Health Service trusts, businesses and individuals who are all committed to suicide prevention in the UK and beyond. The alliance is ultimately concerned with improving support for people contemplating suicide by raising awareness of and promoting FREE suicide prevention training which is accessible to all. The aims of this training are to: enable people to identify when someone is presenting with suicidal thoughts/behaviour, to be able to speak out in a supportive manner, and to empower them to signpost the individual to the correct services or support.

MINDED
themindedtrust.org

The MindEd Trust is a Registered Charity which is focused on the prevention of mental illness in young people and early intervention strategies for those experiencing trauma.
The Trust was established following the tragic death of Edward Mallen, an outstanding young man who took his life on the railway following the inexplicable, rapid and catastrophic onset of severe depression in February 2015.
'We mind what happened to Edward Mallen and we will do all we can to avert similar tragedies through the prevention and alleviation of mental ill-health amongst young people.'
Via mindEducation programmes, we are minded to improve mental health for young people. Key objectives include:

- To promote and assist in the creation of embedded, whole school mental illness prevention and early inter vention programmes throughout the education system.

- To destroy the stigma and guilt associated with mental ill-health so that people experiencing trauma come forward early and openly to seek help. On moral, social and economic grounds, prevention is far better than cure, enhancing resilience and preventing people falling into crisis.

- To actively press for urgent policy and funding reform throughout the education and health system, ensuring that parity of esteem is matched by parity of funding and parity of care.

Registered charity number: 1163922

MALE VOICE ED
www.malevoiced.com

MaleVoicED is a charity providing a platform to all males enabling the sharing of narrative around poor relationships with food and co-morbid conditions.

MaleVoicED also shares the experiences of caregivers, friends and associates who have been affected by such poor food-related relationships.

MaleVoicED hopes that with the sharing of such narratives, services for males will be improved.

Registered charity number: 1139351

ALZHEIMER'S SOCIETY
www.alzheimers.org.uk
0300 222 11 22

Alzheimer's Society is the UK's leading dementia charity. They campaign for change, fund research to find a cure and support people living with dementia today.

Registered charity number: 296645

CRUSE BEREAVEMENT CARE
www.cruse.org.uk

0808 808 1677

Cruse offers face-to-face, telephone, email and website support. They have a Freephone national helpline and local services, and a website (hopeagain.org.uk) specifically for children and young people. Our services are provided by our network of 5,000 trained volunteers and are confidential and free. Cruse also provides training and consultancy for external organisations and for those who may encounter bereaved people in the course of their work.

Registered charity number: 208078

Index